CONTENTS

1 INTRODUCTION

Some years ago, I was a rookie police officer. And, although I got started in law enforcement later in life and should have known better, like most rookie officers my view of law enforcement came from a steady diet of movies and old episodes of COPS on television. Once I put on that starched and pressed uniform, shined my boots and badge, and put on the "Batman" belt full of tools and toys, I made one of the worst mistakes any rookie officer can make: I went into full blown You-Will-Respect-My-Authority mode.

It was bad. No. It was worse than bad. To paraphrase the old cliché, my fat mouth was writing checks my body had a hard time cashing. Any time I was on scene, I was in charge and, by golly, I was going to make sure you knew it. I would talk down to people in the harshest of ways and heaven help them if they talked back to me. In fact, I became such a crap magnet, my peers began calling me Magneto, after the Marvel Comics character. Within a short period of time, my name appeared on more Use of Force reports than practically the rest of the department combined. I had been hit with pepper spray more times than the OC instructor, and it was usually by my own hand (yes, I hate to admit it, but I usually wound up spraying myself.) I had even been taken to the emergency room for fractured ribs, the result of a fight that everyone said I had WON (funny, I sure didn't feel like a winner.)

Needless to say, something had to give. If not, only one of two outcomes were possible. Either I was going to get hurt (or worse!), or I was going to get fired. There's just no other way around it. Thankfully, a veteran officer pulled me aside and said, "Brother, you really gotta learn how to talk to people." And thus began my journey.

I went out and bought every book on police verbal skills I could find. And you know what I found out? Surprisingly, even though it is perhaps one of the most important skills in an officer's toolbox, there were very few books and other resources out there specifically for law enforcement. Want to learn physical defensive tactics? Tons of books, videos, and classes available. Want to learn to shoot better? Even more resources than defensive tactics. Need to learn how to properly talk to people on the street? Sorry. That you mostly have to figure out on your own.

As a result, I sought other resources. I read civilian communication books. I enrolled in a year-long communication course. I even studied sales manuals because, if you think about it, when we are talking to a subject, witness, or suspect, we are usually trying to "sell" them something, are we not? An idea. Cooperation. Sometimes we might just be selling them on not getting their butt whipped or spending the night in jail, but we're still selling something.

Very quickly, my verbal skills improved dramatically. I became quite adept at talking to people and deescalating volatile situations. Soon, less experienced officers began asking me how I did it, and I quietly put together a short PowerPoint presentation. We're talking 5-10 slides here at most. I started sharing it with the officers on my shift and, in turn, they improved.

One day, my supervisor just happened to walk into the room when I was sharing with a junior officer. He didn't say anything. Unbeknownst to me at the time, he sent an email to our Training Division and suggested I share with the entire department. I received a phone call shortly thereafter, asking if I would be interested in teaching my "class" for in-service that year. When I said yes, the response I got almost made me swallow my tongue. He said, "Great! I'll need you to cover about 4 hours' worth of material." Remember, I only had 5-10 slides at this point. So, I did what any intelligent person would do in similar circumstances. I said, "No problem, sir. You can count on me." Then I hung up the phone and panicked.

I hearkened back to my university days and jumped feet first into research and developed a full four-hour course. It proved so successful that I was asked to teach it every month as part of new officer orientation, which I have for nearly four years now at the time of this writing. In fact, I went on to develop a second four-hour course on more advanced techniques, many of which you will learn in this book.

Good luck, and welcome to Tactical Communication.

2 WHAT YOU WILL LEARN

Enough about me. Let's get to the real reason you are here reading this right now. Perhaps you, too, sometimes struggle with communicating with the public. Or, perhaps you are even as bad as I was -- although I can't imagine how that would even be possible -- and you need to change immediately. Either way, you've come to the right place.

In this book, you'll learn how to approach people, open a line of communication, and connect on a level that you may have never experienced before.

You will learn how to deal with difficult people.

You will learn how to talk to the emotionally upset.

You will learn how to handle complaints swiftly and easily.

You will even learn my particular specialty: How to talk to, and more importantly, deescalate mental patients when they begin to "decompensate".

You will learn all this and more.

I promise to hold nothing back and share every tip and technique I know. And here is the key... none of it will be merely theory. Although I will share the theory behind the technique if available, nothing you learn here will be theory alone. Everything presented in this book is field tested by myself and other officers.

I teach it because it works in the street, not just in the classroom. Period.

3 NOTHING NEW

First things first, I'd like to make an honest admission. It has been said that there is nothing new under the sun. That is certainly the case here. I, personally, do not lay claim to any of the tips and techniques you will learn in this book. As you know if you read the introduction, I knew nothing about proper communication when I started. My "expertise", if you will, is simply in my ability to research vast amounts of material, winnow out the fluff, field test what works and what doesn't, and compile the remaining information into something you will hopefully find useful.

When possible, I will give credit where credit is due and let you know where the information came from. Otherwise, just know that I probably picked it up somewhere from someone else as I took my journey. I don't pretend to be the inventor of anything; I'm honestly not that smart. But if there is one thing I learned to do well in graduate school is research and writing (probably the only thing I learned, but that's another story.)

That said, then, please save your negative emails and posts about my lack of creativity. I fully admit up front that it all comes from other experts. But, as my professor once taught me, "To borrow from one is plagiarism, to borrow from many is research."

I tell my classes that they are free to consider me an instructor, a coach, or a mentor, whatever they prefer. What I absolutely am NOT is a guru. I don't have all the answers. Anyone who tells you they do is full of it. Just sayin'.

So, without further ado, let the games begin. See you on the other side.

4 WHAT & WHY

So, what exactly is Tactical Communication?

Well, to begin with, most people know what communication is, even if they can't technically define it. You understand that in order to communicate, you need at least three basic things: a sender, a receiver, and some form of message.

Indeed, strategic coach, Kain Ramsay, suggests that there are actually four levels to communication. What we mean. What we actually say. What the receiver hears. And, perhaps most importantly, the judgments the receiver makes about what he or she thinks we mean. Therefore, as you can see, there is actually much more going on than even the three basic requirements I mentioned.

But what exactly do I mean when I inject the word "tactical"?

One of my instructors at the Academy once quipped that cops are so gullible you could take a dog turd, spray paint it black, and label it tactical and we'd be lined up around the block on payday to buy the damn thing. Not exactly what I mean, but close.

Tactical Communication is the use of specific language, used in specific patterns, designed to achieve a specific result. In other words, it should be thought of as goal-oriented interaction, as opposed to just random, superficial conversations. For example, if you and I are conversing about last night's ball game, or the weather, or going fishing this weekend, we're basically in superficial mode. We're communicating somewhat, of course, but we don't necessarily have an end in mind.

Tactical Communication is far different. Here, you enter into the conversation already armed with a particular outcome you hope to achieve. For instance, if you are dispatched on a disorderly person call, your goal may be to get the person to "calm down" (which, by the way, are two words that you will learn later you should never use!)

Okay, now that you know what it is, exactly why do you need it?

Well, for starters, many times our natural language may actually escalate a situation. If you ask a suspect to stop and talk to you, and he replies, "F***

you, pig!" and your natural reaction is to snatch him up and say, "No, F***
You!" ... do you think that would escalate or deescalate that situation? And
should a situation escalate, is it possible that things could turn physical? And
is that really what you want? I didn't think so.

You see, Tactical Communication is designed to achieve what I call the
primary goal. The primary goal in any potential conflict with a subject should
be voluntary compliance. Think about it this way. As a security or law
enforcement officer, can you make someone do something? Okay, technically
we can't make anyone do anything they don't want to do, but in reality, can a
police officer, in certain circumstances, make someone comply? Yes. If
legally justified, we are afforded the right to impose our will on a subject by
the Fourth Amendment. You may have heard the old three-step process: Ask
'em, Tell 'em, Make 'em.

But again, the question is, does doing so escalate or deescalate that situation?
Of course it escalates. How could it not? Most people simply do not like
being pushed around, regardless of whether they're in the wrong or not. So,
instead, we use Tactical Communication to try and talk them into going along
with whatever it is that we have in mind.

5 WHEN NOT TO USE

Now that I've talked up how powerful and necessary Tactical Communication is, would you believe there are actually times that you should not use it? It's true. There are basically five circumstances where using Tactical Communication may actually lead to much bigger -- and potentially more dangerous -- consequences.

SAFETY/SECURITY RISK

If there is an immediate risk to your safety and security, do not attempt Tactical Communication. For example, if you are in a confrontation with a subject, and he or she pulls a weapon, this is clearly not the time to gently say to this person, "Excuse me, sir. I'm going to have to ask you to place the knife on the floor or I will be forced to speak to you quite harshly." Nope. You must deal with the threat as quickly and efficiently as possible.

ATTACK

Similarly, if some dirt-bag is raining punches down on your beautiful face, this is not a good time to use Tactical Communication. Get your hands up and, as my friend who teaches self-defense is fond of saying, keep the pretty, pretty.

FLIGHT

This one seems like common sense. If a dude takes off running, chances are you're not going to be successful talking him down. One, he's gone. Two, he's likely not listening anyway.

I would like to take a moment here to go slightly off topic. If a suspect does rabbit on you, by all means do your job and chase after him. Please, however, also do yourself a favor. If you lose sight of him for even a few seconds, do your best Fred Flintstone impression to dig those heels into the ground and stop. There are countless stories out there of officers who, in the heat of the moment, let their adrenaline get the best of them. They continued to pursue around a corner or through a door and the suspect was waiting for them, weapon in hand. Don't be a victim.

Okay, back to our regularly scheduled program.

EXCESSIVE REPETITION

What comes to mind when I say excessive repetition? Most officers believe it's when they find themselves repeating commands over and over. And that is certainly one side of the coin. But it works in the opposite direction as well. Sometimes, the person you are speaking to will just say the same thing over and over regardless of what anyone says (The fancy term for this is a "cognitive loop", and you will learn all about it later.)

Once I was dispatched to a call regarding a psychiatric patient who was out of control. When I arrived, I quickly determined she was caught in a loop. No matter what anyone said, her response over and over was, "F*** you, Bitch!" Except for me; then her response was "F*** you, FAT Bitch!" Yes, I'm rather chunky. (I once had a subject I was trying to talk down refer to me as Chris Farley. I had to bite my lip to keep from laughing.)

REVISED PRIORITIES

Finally, we have revised priorities. This just basically means anything not covered by the first four. You're doing something and something more important comes along. A good example might be that you're working on a bit of community-oriented policing and just having a friendly conversation, and all of a sudden your partner starts screaming on the radio for back-up.

Now, notice that the first letter of each of these categories spell out the word SAFER. I believe the SAFER concept was originally developed by George Thompson, author of the classic book, Verbal Judo, but I have seen the idea floated around in many places. By the way, we'll talk more about Dr. Thompson in a bit.

SAFER

Did you know that you are a super hero? Believe it or not, it's true. Every person has a particular super power, and I can prove it. If you have ever read the comic book or seen the movie, Spider-Man, you'll know exactly what I'm talking about. What happens whenever danger begins to happen around our web-slinging hero? Right. His "spidey-sense" begins to tingle. Well, my friend, you have it too.

Have you ever been in a situation and something just didn't feel right? Perhaps you can't even put your finger on it to describe exactly what it is, but you still feel it? You get goosebumps. The hair on the back of your neck and arms begins to stand up. Your gut begins to squirm. You know what I'm talking about. Well, that's your spider sense, and it's usually right.

So, if you can't remember the specific categories of the SAFER concept, just pay attention to your gut instinct. If your sense alarms are going off, you should assume that one or more of the SAFER categories is in play and you need to begin to back out and call for reinforcements.

6 UNIVERSAL TRUTHS

Earlier I mentioned the immortal George Thompson. Dr. Thompson was an English professor that got tired of academia and, oddly enough, quit to become a police officer. He later went on to write perhaps the most well-known book about Tactical Communication ever published. I mentioned Verbal Judo in the last chapter, and if you have been in law enforcement for longer than about eight and a half minutes and not read this book, you have no idea what you're missing. It's fairly short, easy to read, and inexpensive, which makes it all the more baffling that more officers haven't read it.

Thompson outlined what he called his Five Universal Truths. Now, before we go into them one-by-one, let me point something out. My undergraduate degree is in the field of anthropology. Anthropology has several branches, all of which I experienced in my four and a half years, but I focused primarily on the branch known as cultural anthropology. Essentially, I concentrated on various people and their particular culture. Many of my classes consisted of titles like, People of North America, People of Africa, People of the Middles East, etc.

Who cares, right? Well, I certainly don't bring this up to brag, but to impress upon you the power of Thompson's truths. Having studied a multitude of cultures around the world, I can assure you that he is dead on. It doesn't matter if you are talking to someone from Texas or Timbuktu, Anchorage or the Amazon, Milwaukee or Moscow, these principles apply to everyone.

Let me say this, however. As an anthropologist, the only challenge I have is with the first one. It is not that Thompson was wrong. Far from it. It's just that he didn't elaborate enough.

NUMBER ONE: PEOPLE WANT TO BE TREATED WITH DIGNITY AND RESPECT.

This is certainly true. Don't you? Aren't you far more receptive to a person who is treating you with a level of respect and maintaining your dignity, instead of talking to you like you're the scum of the earth?

So where is the challenge? Well, it is important to keep in mind that different cultures have different definitions of what exactly constitutes dignity and respect. For instance, in the West, we are taught that you should always look someone in the eye when you are speaking to them. In fact, if you look away or stare at the floor, what do we usually interpret that to mean? Exactly. The person may be untrustworthy, dishonest, or flat out lying. Regardless, it is most definitely seen as a sign of disrespect.

On the other hand, in many Asian and some Middle Eastern cultures, it is exactly the opposite. For them, making direct eye contact is a sign of disrespect. Due to the hierarchal nature of their society, to look directly at a person higher on the social scale means you are challenging his or her authority. Thus, children are taught at an early age to avert the eyes of a "superior".

Can you see how this is important? Understanding this idea, do you think it would make a difference on how you interpret a situation depending on the cultural background of the person you are speaking to? Keep this in mind.

NUMBER TWO: PEOPLE WANT TO BE ASKED, NOT ORDERED.

Again, don't you prefer it when someone asks you to do something as opposed to telling, commanding, or demanding? This is often a tough one to remember because, let's face it, most police departments are set up in a quasi-military fashion, meaning it is quite common for higher officers to just bark orders at their team. Forget that this is just a poor model of leadership for a moment -- I will soon be coming out with a book on this very topic, by the way -- but it is easy to fall in the trap of speaking to the public this way as well, and most civilians respond to it about as well as you might expect; which means they don't respond well at all.

NUMBER THREE: PEOPLE WANT TO BE TOLD WHY.

Oh my goodness, how true this one is. Remember when you were a tiny toddler? Every time Mom or Dad said something to you, what did you say? "Why?" ... "Why?" ... "Why?" It was enough to drive Mom to drinking, right? The funny thing is we all believe that we outgrew that behavior when we got out of diapers. But, naturally, we didn't. I don't care if you're two, twenty, or two-hundred and twenty, you still want to know the reason why when someone asks you to do something.

NUMBER FOUR: PEOPLE WANT TO BE GIVEN OPTIONS.

My department is big on community-oriented policing. In fact, we focus on good community relations so much that I often half-jokingly state that if you are in the back of one of our patrol cars and on your way to jail, you have really screwed up. What I mean is that we will give a person chance after chance, option after option, to come up with an alternative.

Now, before you scoff, admit it; you probably do it, too. After all, booking someone in is kind of a pain in the ass, and don't get me started on the mountain of paperwork that follows. Here's a test.

Which option would you prefer?

1) You could have a friend or family member take an intoxicated individual home and keep an eye on him until he sobers up.

-Or-

2) You can wrestle him into the car, listen to him swear like a sailor in Singapore, fight to get him into booking, fill out half a dozen forms, wait forever at the back of the line for the judge (who, for some reason, is always on lunch no matter what time you arrive), and best of all, spend the next 30 minutes cleaning up the vomit in your back seat and the next 12 hours trying to air out the damn stench.

Yeah, I agree. I'd go with option one every time, too.

NUMBER FIVE: PEOPLE WANT A SECOND CHANCE.

Call me a cock-eyed optimist (or terribly naive), but I truly believe that there is a good person deep down inside most everyone. And I agree with Thompson wholeheartedly. Everyone wants a second chance. Even the "bad guys".

Where I work the number one crime by far is theft. One night I was dispatched to a suspicious person call. Like most police officers, a common question I ask is if the person has ever been in trouble with the law before. The suspect said that he had actually done jail time in the past. When I asked what for, he said theft. Remember our discussion on the SAFER concept?

Given that this is our biggest problem, what do you think my spider sense was doing at that moment? Exactly. I was buzzing like a fly at the windowsill on a bright sunny day. But let me ask you a question: had I reacted to this information alone, and began treating him like a criminal, do you think I would have escalated or deescalated the situation? I hope by now you know the answer.

Instead, regardless of my natural instinct, I understood Thompson's truth. So I asked when he had been in jail. This man was 44 years old. He had served time when he was 19. Oh, and he'd had a clean record ever since. So, what do you think? Do you believe he was looking for a second chance?

7 HOW TO APPROACH PEOPLE

One of the hardest things for inexperienced officers -- and even for many veterans -- is how to approach people. I don't necessarily mean that you see something wrong and you react; we all seem to do that pretty well. Here, I'm talking more about the community-oriented policing concept. Just how do we walk up to essentially random strangers and begin a conversation?

I've tried quite a few methods, but the one I have found to be the best is a modified version of the 8-step process outlined by our old friend, George Thompson.

There are several key ideas that you have to keep in mind. First, this process is basically used to make contact the first time you meet someone. As you will soon see, it would be a bit awkward to use all eight steps every time you came in contact. It is also important that you follow the steps in the order in which they are written. Each step serves a specific purpose and is where it is for a specific reason. And, finally, though it should go without saying, you want to make sure that you are always friendly and courteous.

STEP 1

When you approach someone for the first time, you should begin with some form of introductory greeting. At this stage, you want to keep things relatively formal. For instance, "Good morning, Sir," or "Good day, Ma'am," work well. As I mentioned, you want to be friendly, but you don't really want to appear too familiar. In other words, you wouldn't approach them like someone you went to high-school with (unless, of course, you did!)

Another good greeting might be, "Excuse me. May I speak with you for a minute?" It's polite, and it gets to the point of why you are approaching them in the first place rather quickly. You need to be careful, however, and not delay too long before you move to the next step. Think about what might be going through their mind. A police officer just walked up, said he needs to talk to them, and then... dead silence. I don't know about you, but if it were me in that situation I would immediately hear Scooby Doo's voice in my head: Ruh-Roh!

STEP 2

Go ahead and introduce yourself. Identify who you are and who you work for. For example, "I'm officer Smith with the Metropolitan Police Department." Don't be one of those jerk officers who skips this step because you think they should know who you are because, after all, you're wearing a uniform and a name tag. Instead, the burden is on you to identify yourself. Besides, you should consider this just common courtesy anyway.

Step 3

In this step, you want to explain the reason for contact. Keep it simple. I usually say something like, "The reason I'm talking to you is _____." There are two primary reasons for this. One, do you remember the universal truths we discussed earlier? This helps answer that universal "why?" question. More importantly for you, however, is that this acts as a form of safety check.

Why are traffic stops so dangerous? It's primarily because you have no idea what you're walking up to, right? Same idea here. Let's say for example that this person murdered his entire family with an ax this morning. And, on his way to Canada, he decided to stop in your jurisdiction for some reason. When you walk up in your fancy uniform and start talking to him, what's he thinking? "Oh, crap! They must have found the bodies." Who knows what this fool might do at this point?

But what if you say, "The reason I'm talking to you is that I saw you looking around sort of confused. Is there anything I can help you find?" Now what's he thinking? Probably something like, "Whew... they don't know yet." The point is that he will be less likely to shift into fight or flight mode if he thinks he's gotten away with whatever he's hiding.

Step 4

Here you just want to ask any applicable questions based on the information you have so far. For instance, you might ask how you could be of assistance. Is there anything you can do to help? And so on. Keep it light and friendly, but pay attention to their body language and demeanor, as well as how and what they are saying. Are you picking up any inconsistencies based on the circumstances, like overly nervous, constantly looking around, etc.?

Step 5

At this point, if the situation warrants it, I will ask for some form of verification. I might ask to see an ID, a driver's license, a visitor's pass, etc. The key here is to make it a bit soft and nonchalant, almost as if it's an afterthought. If you've ever seen an old episode of Columbo, you get the idea. I usually go with something like, "Oh, by the way, since we're here, would you happen to have your ID on you?" Make it appear like it's no big deal.

STEP 6

Step six is an important one. It is officially called the clarification step, but I call it Liar's Poker. It goes like this: "So... what brings you to ______?"

First, notice the hesitation after the word "So". In communication, inserting what is called a pregnant pause -- a pause slightly longer than usual, say about a beat and a half -- is very effective at gaining attention. When you hesitate like that, people tend to perk up, sort of like a dog's ears when you say its name. Then, once you have asked the question, comes the most important part. You must, absolutely, positively, SHUT UP!

Seriously. Just stop talking and listen. Because what's the problem with a lie? You gotta remember that sucker, right? And most people who are being dishonest are making it up as they go along. To be brutally honest, most people simply aren't smart enough to keep track of all those details on the fly like that. So, he says that he's here visiting his cousin, Jeffery, who lives at 123 Maple Lane. A few minutes later you say, "Okay, just to make sure I heard you correctly, you're here to see your brother, Johnny, who lives at 321 Staple Place, correct?" If he agrees, you know you have a problem.

Also, did you notice that the false details you feed back are relatively close in length, cadence, and sound? Instead of Jeffery it's Johnny. 321 instead of 123. Place, not Lane. Even cousin and brother share two sound beats each: cou-sin, bro-ther. The reason for this is that if you make your details too different -- like replacing Jeffery with Bob, for instance -- he may not remember exactly what he said, but he'll have a vague idea that it didn't sound like that. Remember, bad guys have spider sense, too.

STEP 7

There's not really a script for this one, at least not one that you would use on the subject. It's really more of an internal script, if you will. You just think about what your next move is. Does everything check out? Do they seem legit? Or, do you need to start getting back-up heading your way?

STEP 8

At this point, you are going to use an appropriate closing statement based on the decision you made in step seven. If there is nothing to be concerned with, you might say something like, "It was nice meeting you. Please let me know if you need anything." If you feel the need to issue a bit of admonishment, you might try something like, "In the future, I suggest you ______. Your safety is my primary concern."

But what if things are feeling funny? Maybe you can't even put your finger on anything specifically, but your spider sense is sounding alarm bells and your gut is rolling. How might you go about calling for support?

Obviously, the wrong answer is to just come right out and say it. Think about it. If you're standing right in front of a suspect, and you get on the radio and say, "Start me another unit this way," what kind of reaction might he have? Do you think this might escalate things just a bit? Of course it would, particularly if he's got something to hide (like, say, a dead family back home.)

What about your 10 Codes? After all, that's the whole reason the department has them, right? So that no one knows what we're talking about? Ah, but therein lies the challenge; they have no idea what you're talking about. So, let's say that you want to go eat lunch with George as soon as you wrap up this call. So you get on the radio and call George about a 10-95 (or whatever code your department uses.) But if a suspect is standing there, and especially if he's hiding something, what's he going to think? Even though you and George know a 95 is lunch, don't you think the bad guy is going to assume the worst? Of course. And when he does, is that situation likely to escalate? You know it will.

Well, then, if that is the case, how in the world do we call for back-up without setting off alarm bells? I'm glad you asked. It took several months of trial and error to develop this next script. Once perfected, however, it has proved to be very useful in the field for several years now.

It does not matter if you have worked for your department for three hours, thirty days, three months, or thirty years, you now have my permission to lie like a dog. All you have to do is put on your "rookie" mask. You say something like, "I'm sorry, sir. I apologize. I just (started with this department, transferred to this unit, moved to this part of the city, whatever), and I'm not really familiar with that. Let me get someone over here that can help you."

The beauty of this technique is that they think that you are actually getting someone that could potentially help them, even if the "help" they need is a lie on their part. But you and I really know who's coming, don't we? That's right: The Calvary.

So, there you have it. How to approach people in a nut-shell. I encourage you to take these steps, and the accompanying scripts, and work on them until they become quite natural.

8 WHAT IS CONFLICT?

What exactly is conflict? Is it merely a disagreement, or is it something more?

Think about your favorite ice cream. Since there is no way for you to share that with me, let's say for the sake of argument that it is vanilla, since this appears to be the most popular flavor. Now, my favorite flavor is chocolate. And Barbara's favorite is strawberry. Is there any conflict between the three of us? Not really. While we all might have a preference, we really couldn't care less what flavor the other likes; it's just a difference of opinion.

But what if my wife and I wish to go to the movies? She wants to go see the latest "chick flick", and I want to go see stuff get blown up. Both movies start in five minutes, and neither of us want to see a movie alone. Is there conflict there? You betcha.

So what's the difference between these two scenarios?

Communication expert, William Wilmot, once defined conflict as, "An expressed struggle between at least two interdependent parties who perceive incompatible goals, scarce resources, and interference from others in achieving their goals." The key word is interdependent. You see, when we were discussing ice cream, there was no interdependence in our goals. As long as there is enough ice cream to go around, we don't experience any conflict.

But in the movie example, there is clearly more than just preference. First, though not required, in this case there was a relationship, one form of interdependence. Did we have incompatible goals that interfered with one another? Of course. In fact, there was even a type of scarcity as well in that both movies were about to start.

Thus, in order to understand conflict, you need to realize that it is obviously more than mere disagreement. Also, it is important to know that conflict will continue if ignored. It will just sit there, simmering, bubbling just under the surface, until one day one of you can't take the pressure any more and... BOOM!

Conflict will often trigger extremely strong emotions. When people are passionate about something, they often experience a visceral reaction, meaning that there are some deep-rooted feelings inside that they feel physically that will not go away.

Perhaps the most important concept to grasp for the purposes of conflict resolution is this: a person's response to a situation is often based on perceptions, not on actual fact.

9 WHAT'S YOUR COLOR?

Let's put communication on hold for just a minute. Instead, let's talk about perception.

When I was in college, I studied the great philosophers. One in particular that really fascinated me was a character named Ludwig Wittgenstein. He worked primarily in the areas of logic, (the philosophy of) mathematics, and for our purposes, language.

Wittgenstein believed that the limits of one's language can limit their world. He developed an argument commonly known as Wittgenstein's Beetle, or the Beetle in a Box theory. Without getting into too much gobbledeegook that philosophy is so well known for, the basic idea is as follows.

Let's say that there are several of us sitting around, and each is handed a shoe box that they are told contains a beetle. Now, each is asked to describe what their beetle looks and acts like. But there is a catch. No one is allowed to look into anyone else's box. The question then, Wittgenstein argued, is how can we be sure that as you describe your beetle, it is the same thing as mine?

What he meant was that we are merely using a string of words to describe something. And these words may or may not be related to what is actually in our box. In fact, our box may even be empty, containing no beetle whatsoever. In essence, this string of words are simply symbols that may be describing a different insect, a rock, a sock, or even nothing at all. We have no way of knowing because we can't see into your box.

Okay, now that I have completely confused you, what the heck does this have to do with perception?

I want you to conduct a little experiment. Grab an item. It doesn't really matter what it is. Now, ask yourself what color that object is. Take that object around to several other people and ask them what color it is. What results did you get? Did everyone agree? Good.

Now consider this. What happens if you look at that item and say that it's red. You show it around to three or four other people and they all say it's red. So far, so good. But when we get to Charles we run into a problem. You ask Charles what color he sees and he replies, "Blue." Here's the million-dollar question: Who's the crazy one?

Forget Charles for a moment. Think about everyone else. You can't see into their heads and they can't see into yours. The fact may be that when you look at the item, you actually see brown. The others see yellow, green, and pink. So how can everyone "see" red? The answer may surprise you. It is this: all of your life, people have pointed to this particular color vibration and said, "That's red." So regardless of what each person actually sees, they all say red. Thus, reality is simply what we all agree that it is.

Whoa! Wait a minute, home boy. Are you saying that there is no such thing as reality? No. I'm not saying that there is nothing "out there" (although there are some philosophers who argue that very idea.) What Wittgenstein and I are saying is that since the only connection we have is our words, what's out there is what we agree is out there. This is an extremely important concept to grasp if you hope to improve your communication. Taken to the extreme, we can look at the example of a patient experiencing mental issues.

Robert has been admitted to the hospital for schizophrenic tendencies. He insists that he hears voices telling him to harm himself and other people. He also talks to Timmy, a young boy about six years old, with blue hair, who sits in the corner of the room. Now you and I know that Timmy and the voices aren't real. After all, we can't see or hear them. Therefore, Robert must be crazy, right? But in a sense, he's not, because he actually does see and hear them.

Always remember this:

Just because you do not agree with another person's "reality" does not mean it does not exist for them.

10 POSITIVE INTENTIONS

What if I told you that no matter what a person does, behind every behavior is a positive intention?

Did I say some behavior? Nope. I said every behavior. Neuro-linguistic programming (NLP) trainer, Tom Hoobyar, proposed that, "No matter how weird or inappropriate it may seem, for that person there is an inner logic that makes perfect sense." I know, at first it can be hard to wrap your mind around an idea like this. But think about it.

I'm sure you would agree that Adolf Hitler was perhaps the most disgusting human being to ever breath oxygen. I mean, most people equate him with evil incarnate, right? But is that how Hitler saw himself? Not a chance. He considered himself a hero. He was, he would argue, simply trying to save his country. In fact, he would wonder how he could not do what he did. Like Hoobyar said, old Dolf's inner logic made perfect sense to him.

(By the way, before I receive tons of hate mail, I absolutely do NOT condone what Hitler did. In fact, I am one of those who actually does consider him the embodiment of evil. I only use him as an example for the idea of positive intention because he is arguably the most extreme case available.)

So when you are communicating with a person, try and remember that he or she is saying and doing things only because they believes it is in their best interest.

11 DEALING WITH DIFFICULT PEOPLE

Before we get too deep into dealing with difficult people, let's go over rule number one.

You must never, ever, under any circumstances, get upset.

Ha! I couldn't even write that sentence with a straight face. Let's face it (no pun intended), this is by far easier said than done, right? I remember one time I was dealing with this guy and he was being particularly cranky. This was years ago, and yet to this day I have no idea what he said or did that set me off. All I remember is losing my cool and my partner stepping in and separating us before things got physical.

Nevertheless, you have to try your best to not let this happen. Our old friend, George Thompson, once quipped that arguing with an angry person is like trying to win an argument with your dog. I don't know about you, but I haven't had much luck with that.

One way to keep this in check is to remember that everyone listens to the same radio station. That's right. It's call sign is WII-FM: What's In It For Me?

Whenever you are dealing with difficult people try to keep this in mind. They really only want to know one thing. What's in it for them? Therefore, what you want to do is explain the benefits of cooperation early. Let them know what they are going to get out of the deal if they cooperate. It's also important to answer their questions, especially the "why".

You don't want to dismiss their questions. That will generally only escalate the situation. But that does not necessarily mean you need to answer them in that moment. If it's reasonably safe to do so, it's okay to delay. One trick that I've had more success with than not is to say to a person that's being particularly loud or angry is, "Sir, I want to answer all of your questions, but not like this. Would you mind bringing it down a notch so we can discuss how I might help you?" Remember I said reasonably safe. If your gut is telling you you're about to get punched in the face, you might want to try something else.

12 THE DISTURBANCE SET

What follows is the longest, and arguably the most important, chapter in this entire book. I call it the Disturbance Set. It consists of a series of techniques that are designed to deescalate a situation as efficiently as possible.

It's important to note that my definition of a difficult person is one that is escalating, cursing, speaking loudly, angry, etc. I don't mean someone who is experiencing emotional distress like sadness or grief. We'll discuss that later.

The steps, in order, are the:

Wedge

Intermission

End Run

Turnaround

Key

Anchor

The Wedge

What do we use a wedge for? Think about a wedge you might use to hold open a door or pry two things apart. Basically, we are using it to create some form of opening.

One thing you absolutely must understand upfront is that the Wedge is an extremely aggressive technique. Used by itself I can almost guarantee that it will escalate a situation, and even potentially get you into a physical altercation.

Why use it then?

Unfortunately, sometimes you have no other choice. If you walk up on a scene and a person is borderline out of control, you likely won't get anywhere by speaking in a soft, low voice. The sad fact is that politeness will often not cut through the person's agitated brain.

Thus, you can think of this one as optional and use it only as needed.

Repeat after me...

"Whoa, whoa, whoa... Time out."

As you say time out, bring your hands up into a T position in front of your upper body (the classic "time out" gesture.) This does two things for you. First, most people recognize the T symbol, so it gives a clear visual cue that associates with your words. More importantly, it forces you to get your hands up. If this person is going to attempt something physical, like a grab or assault, wouldn't you prefer to have your hands up in order to defend yourself?

The Intermission

What's an intermission? It's a break. A pause. A hiccup in time. And that's exactly what we are looking for. We're trying to buy ourselves a little time so we can talk to this person.

Remember when I said the Wedge is a very aggressive technique? The way you overcome that is to jump immediately into the intermission. And I do mean immediately. You cannot pause for even a second.

First, the intermission:

Repeat...

"I'm here to help."

At the same time, you take your hands from the T position and turn them outward toward the person, palms facing them, like you would if you were pushing open a door. You can even gently shrug your shoulders a bit. In defensive tactics, this is called the passive stance. It's very non-threatening. But combined with your interview stance, it's very deceptive.

While it looks very passive, the reality is that there is no difference between the passive stance and balling your fists up in a fighting stance. No difference, that is, except what witnesses see. In fact, I argue that it is more effective anyway, should a fight break out. The last thing you want is to experience what is known as a boxer's fracture and break your hand. Not only does it make it difficult to fight, it makes it darn near impossible to draw your weapon. Not good. But that is exactly what is going to happen if you accidentally connect the small bones in your fist with that giant bowling ball on the subject's shoulders that we call a head. Keep 'em open.

So, combined with the Wedge, it would look something like this:

"Whoa, whoa, whoa... Time out (while making a T symbol). I'm here to help." Passive stance.

Got it? Good.

THE END RUN

In football, an End Run is an attempt by the ball carrier to run around the end of the defensive line rather than running directly up the middle of the field. The challenge with a direct attempt is that there is an entire army of linemen waiting to crush you. By running around them, you have a better chance at accomplishing your goal.

Likewise, in communication, an End Run is an attempt to circumvent the discussion for the moment. It is literally an attempt to "run around" a subject's current emotions. For instance, if a person is angry and proving to be difficult, addressing their emotions directly may actually escalate the situation.

The End Run is quite simple really. All you are doing is essentially agreeing with the person and acknowledging his or her issue.

The first End Run is the phrase, "I understand." Now, this common phrase is rather tricky. In fact, I call this one a "Danger" Phrase since it can get you into trouble very quickly (By the way, we will not be discussing how to fix it until we get to the section on Danger Phrases, so stay tuned.)

The rest of the End Runs are just variations of agreement and acknowledgment, such as:

"I hear you."

"I got it."

"It certainly seems that way."

"I agree."

"You're right."

Let's talk about the last one for a minute. "You're right," are two of the most powerful words in the English language. We all love to be right, don't we?

So the real question is, can you tell someone they are right if they are right? Of course you can. Can you tell someone they are right if they are wrong? A bit harder, but most of us can do it. But, what if, through some form of righteousness or morality, you just can't bring yourself to tell a person they are right... can you still do it?

Yes. And I'll show you how.

When I say, "You're right," what do you assume I mean? If you are like most people, you believe I mean that you are correct. But English is a funny language, and words can have multiple meanings. We're going to use that fact in our favor.

Your brain has two hemispheres: a left "brain" and a right "brain". The left hemisphere is the realm of logic and reasoning. The right hemisphere is where creativity and emotion live.

When a person is being difficult, most often they are operating from the right hemisphere. They are letting emotions control their thinking. Naturally this can lead to some challenges.

So, when I say, "You're right," they assume I mean they are correct. And more often than not, they will begin to deescalate. But what I am really doing is creating a reminder for myself. I am essentially saying, "You're living in the right hemisphere, and I've got to get you left." Thus, it's a win-win technique for both of us.

It's a subtle difference, but an important one.

The Turnaround

What is a turnaround? They're more common than you might think.

Consider a cul-de-sac. You are driving along in one direction, reach the end, and loop back around to go the opposite direction.

Tactical communication has a similar technique. You've arrived on scene, used the process to get the person to take it down a notch or two. At some point, however, you have to turn the discussion around. The subject has had time to vent and decompress, and now it is time to turn the conversation towards what you need to say.

The turnaround is so simple you will probably laugh. It is literally one simple word:

"... and ..."

Sandwiched between the End Run and the Key (the next technique we will discuss), it works like this. "I hear you. I got it. And what I'm asking is..."

Simple, right?

Okay. Easy enough. What about some alternatives?

How about "but"? Can we use it instead?

Yes and no. "But" has a particular quality that works in some situations and may actually escalate others. Let me give you an example.

I say to a woman, "Sally, you are quite beautiful. And after work, I would like to buy you a drink." Most women would see that as a form of compliment, right?

On the other hand, I begin the same way, changing only the Turnaround. "Sally, you are quite beautiful. But..." OUCH!

Can you see the difference? When I use "and", the conversation keeps moving in a positive direction. When I insert "but", poor Sally is waiting for the other shoe to drop. In fact, some women may even react with, "But!?!? What do you mean, but!?!?" One word potentially gets me a date. The other gets me a black eye.

How about "however"? While it works well in a written setting, such as academic papers and whatnot, I personally don't recommend it in verbal communication. It just comes off as a .75 cent college version of "but".

Stick with "and" as much as you can.

THE KEY

As you know, we use keys to open things. Thus, the "Key" in Tactical Communication is used to open their mind to alternatives. Alternatives to what, you ask? Alternatives to their current behavior.

To use the Key, you want to use a phrase that subtly begins moving the person's behavior into a new direction. It goes like this:

"What I'd like you to do is..."

"What I'm asking you to do is..."

"I'm hoping we can resolve the situation by..."

"Would you mind...?"

And so on. You can see how all the steps begin to flow into one another. You've got your foot in the door, allowed the person to vent his or her frustrations a little, hit 'em with a Turnaround, and now you begin to move them in the direction you need them to go.

Simple.

Bonus Technique: Compliment the Crazy

Speaking of alternatives to behavior, now is a good time to go over one of my favorite, and most effective, techniques. I learned this little gem from one of the top communication experts on the planet, Dan O'Connor. You can find him at his site, www.OnlineCommunicationTraining.com (This is also where you can find the year-long communication course I mentioned in the introduction.)

I don't know Dan well enough to call him a friend (although I would certainly love to someday), but we have exchanged emails on a few occasions. And I can say without hesitation that he is as close to genius as I have ever experienced. Yes, his material is that damn good! By the way, I receive no compensation from him for saying these things. In fact, he barely knows I exist and doesn't know I'm including this. Do yourself a favor and go check out his site. You won't be disappointed. Anyway...

One time I was dispatched to a disorderly person call at the burn unit of the hospital. When I arrived, the nurse was arguing with an extremely pissed off mother. Mom had gone out to run errands and left her child with a sitter. When the sitter put a pot on the stove to prepare lunch... well, I'm sure you can fill in the rest.

Dan's Compliment the Crazy technique is based on the idea that you get what you reward. If you ask Billy to clean his room and all he does is pick up one sock, you basically have two choices. You can beat his butt, or you can pat his head. Punishing someone, or what we call negative reinforcement, will get you compliance. What that means is that you will get the behavior you are seeking, but only as long as you are around. Billy might clean his room because he knows you're watching, but what about when you go out of town? Not a chance.

Instead, most behavioral psychologists recommend positive reinforcement. You ask Billy to clean his room. He picks up one sock. This time you give Billy a high-five and say, "Good job, buddy." How does this make Billy feel? Feels good, right? And Billy, like most of us, likes to feel good. So, tomorrow you ask him to clean his room. This time he picks up one sock -- and his shoes. "Good job, buddy." High-five. Pretty soon, Billy is cleaning his entire room, whether you are standing over him or not, because he has learned to associate pleasure to cleaning his room. It makes him feel good.

Back to the story...

I arrived at the burn unit and saw the nurse arguing with mom. Mom was understandably upset. After all, her daughter was in pain. To make matters worse, mom arrived at the hospital shortly after the child was moved to the burn unit. The fact was that the doctors were still assessing the situation, and she was not going to be allowed to see her daughter for some time. But that is not what the nurse was telling her. Instead, she simply kept repeating, "You can't go back now."

I approach mom, telling the nurse to go back inside, and I start the Disturbance Set. I start with the Wedge, and move straight into the Intermission. I ask mom to tell me what is going on and she tells me the story. Now watch carefully. As she is telling me what happened, I say to her, "I'm surprised you're not even more upset. I've got three kids of my own, and if that happened to one of them, I would be freaking out right now. In fact, I'm impressed you're keeping it together as well as you are."

Now, was she upset? Of course. Was she freaking out? Naturally. Was she keeping it together? Not even close. But what happened? As soon as I said it, she began to relax. Why?

I believe it is for two reasons. First, it's the positive reinforcement principle. I'm rewarding her for the behavior I was looking for, not for the behavior I was currently getting. Second, it showed empathy. Finally, she had someone who was willing to listen to her. (Remember the radio station?) Once she had an open ear to hear and a shoulder to cry on, instead of someone putting road blocks in her way, she felt safe.

The Anchor

Have you ever bought a new car? What typically happens? The salesperson has gone through the pitch and now it's time for the proverbial rubber to meet the road. He leans across the desk and says, "Hmmm... that's a great deal. In fact, I honestly don't even know if I can get that one approved. But let me ask you this. I'm going to go in the back and talk to my manager. And if, by some miracle, I can get his okay on this, are you ready to buy this car today?"

Of course, if you're at all interested in the car, you are probably going to say yes. Maybe even nod your head a bit. Unfortunately for your bank account for the next five years, he's got you right where he wants you. So, he goes in the back to, ahem... talk to the manager. (I used to sell cars. Do you think we're really back there talking to a manager? Nope. Most of the time we're just drinking coffee.) Then he comes back all excited and says, "Wow! Well, I've got some good news. The old man must have forgot to take his meds this morning or something, but he actually approved us. So, if you'll go ahead and drop your John Hancock on that line right there, I'll have the boys give her a good wash and bring her around with a full tank of gas."

Now, let me ask you this. At this point, have you signed anything? No, you have not. So, CAN you still back out of the deal? Of course you can. But WILL you back out of the deal? Not likely. And the reason why might come as a bit of a surprise.

You see, most people generally see themselves as honest. In fact, our self-image practically demands that we don't see ourselves as hypocrites. Therefore, you can still back out of the deal because there is nothing legally binding to prevent you from doing so. However, do you remember what the salesperson did before he walked out? That's right... he "anchored" your agreement. In a sense, you gave him your word that if he got it approved you would buy the car. And he did just that. To back out now would make you feel like a hypocrite, right?

Okay, I'll admit that, used in this way, the Anchor seems rather slimy. Nevertheless, it is still a powerful technique. And used properly, for the purposes of de-escalation, we can use it in Tactical Communication and it works extremely well.

First, here's how it goes:

"Sound good?"

"How's that sound?"

Or, my personal favorite...

"Will you work with me?"

Think about how effective this is when you put all the steps together in order. It goes something like this...

"Whoa, whoa, whoa... time out. I'm here to help. I can see that you're upset. Tell me what's going on. <subject vents>. Okay, I got it. And what I'm asking you to do is to sit down quietly over here and let me work on resolving this for you. Will you work with me?"

If the subject says no, then you just circle back around to one of the earlier steps until you uncover the real issue. But for now, let's assume he or she said yes. Thinking back to our car sales example, if a person agrees to work with you, CAN he or she escalate again when you walk away? Naturally. However, WILL he or she escalate? Not likely, for exactly the same reason; he or she does not want to feel like a hypocrite.

Can you see now just how powerful the Disturbance Set is? I promise that if you take the time to memorize the steps and commit the scripts to memory, you will be amazed at how quickly and effectively you can de-escalate a difficult person.

13 UNDERSTANDING PERSONALITY TYPES

There are many different so-called personality systems out there. I've studied most of them. Some break people down into nine categories, 12 categories, etc. Heck, I even came across one that claimed as many as forty different personality types. While most were fairly accurate, I think that such programs are simply too complicated for use in the field the way we need to; after all, we can't give subjects a written test on the street. Therefore, I prefer a simple, four-category system that I learned from Dan O'Connor.

Before we get too far into the details, it's important to understand that no one personality type is any better or worse than any other. They're all just different. And my research seems to indicate that your particular personality is pretty much set by the time you reach around seven or eight years old. In other words, it's a result of the environment you grew up in. Each type has both strengths and weaknesses which we will cover.

The first personality type is known as Expressive. An Expressive tends to be the type of person who likes to be the center of attention (in a good way.) These would be your teachers, coaches, actors, comedians, etc. Expressives like to perform -- hence the name -- and they generally do it well. Their motto in life would be something like "let's celebrate and have fun."

As you might imagine, an Expressive's strengths include things like communication, a high level of enthusiasm, and they tend to be fairly determined when they are working on something they care about.

But not everything is peaches and cream for an Expressive.

For instance, they often tend to talk too much. And, because it's hard to get them to shut up, they can come across as overbearing at times. And they are dreamers. For example, I am an Expressive, and my unrealistic "dreams" have sometimes landed me in hot water. My wife says that I am an excellent starter, but I'm a lousy finisher. I struggle with focus and I get bored easily, so it's nothing for me to take up a hobby like, say, photography, only to decide three months (and $3000!) later, "Meh... it's not really my thing." My wife wants to strangle me all the time.

Next we have our Amiables. These are our teddy bears. An Amiable is what I like to call people-people. They love people; so much so that their motto might be, "Let's all be friends." Their strengths include things like patience and diplomacy. They usually take support roles. For example, you will tend to find a lot of Amiable types working in positions like nursing or customer service.

But like anyone else, Amiables have some pretty powerful weaknesses, too. Conformity is a big one. An Amiable personality will almost always go along to get along. Put simply, they don't really like to rock the boat. As a result, they often struggle with being assertive. In fact, if you are dealing with an Amiable, you will typically have to pull their real thoughts out of them, almost like pulling teeth from an alligator.

To see what I mean, a conversation with an Amiable might go something like this:

You ask, "So, what do you think, Bob?"

"Sounds good to me," Bob replies.

"Hmmm... it seems like you might have some concerns."

"No. I'm good with it."

"Are you sure? You look like something's bothering you."

"Well, since you asked, I really think..."

You see how you have to push the issue and do a little more digging to get to Bob's real concerns?

The third personality type is what is called the Analytical. Like the name suggests, these are the analytical type people who are all about facts and figures (in fact, that could be considered their motto: just the facts.)

Analyticals are good to have around. They have some very good strengths that a lot of us lack. For instance, they are very detail-oriented thinkers. They are thorough, often leaving no stone unturned. And they are some of the most disciplined people you will ever meet.

Of course, such strengths can lead to severe weaknesses in the opposite. For example, an Analytical will generally exclude feelings. You can't really quantify how someone feels and put it on a spreadsheet, so for an Analytical it's a non-factor. They also tend to be perfectionists, wanting everything to go perfectly according to plan. They do not like surprises. And finally, Analyticals are often too rigid, particularly with rules and procedures. They tend to be on/off, black/white thinkers, with very little tolerance for gray areas.

Finally we have the Drivers. Chances are if you're reading these words right now you are in some form of law enforcement or security. And, that being the case, I can assure you that you have met your fair share of Driver personalities. This kind of work attracts Drivers like pollen to a swarm of bees. And most of the time they do well in such a field. Their strengths include things like being independent and being determined. They are also extremely decisive and never have a problem making a decision, even if that decision is questioned by everyone else. A Driver will almost always stick to their guns unless you can prove otherwise.

Weaknesses. Yeah, they got 'em, too, even if they'll never admit it. Communication skills are generally a huge weakness for a Driver. For example, an Expressive might come up to you and say, "Howdy, John. How's the family? Great. Say... how's that report I asked for coming along?"

A Driver will be a completely different experience. He or she might simply walk up to your desk, hover over you, and say, "Report?" And generally he or she is only looking for a short answer to the question, not some long, drawn out explanation. The boss says, "Report?" You reply, "Three O'Clock." That's an entire conversation for a Driver.

EXPLAINING THE AXES

Once you grasp the four master personality types you are in a position to understand how they interrelate with one another. The categories are based on a set of four characteristics.

The first two characteristics we will consider is openness. In other words, are you more of an open type person, or would you consider yourself more self-contained? Expressives and Amiables are both very "open" type people. They are outgoing and friendly, and like to be around people. Alternatively,

Drivers and Analyticals are more self-contained. They are more reserved, and usually like to be left alone more often than not.

The next set of characteristics is how direct a person is. In this case, the personality types break the other way. Expressives and Drivers are more direct in their approach, whereas Amiables and Analyticals are more indirect in how they deal with people.

If you were to set up a grid with one personality in each corner, it would look something like this:

EXPRESSIVE	AMIABLE
DRIVER	ANALYTICAL

The way it works is that any two personalities that connect in a horizontal or vertical way tend to have much lower conflict because of those common shared traits we talked about. For instance, Driver and Analytical share the self-contained characteristic, so they can relate to one another. The same can be said with Expressive and Amiable since they are both open type people.

Likewise, it works the other direction as well. Expressives and Drivers get along because they are both direct. Amiable and Analytical work well together because they are both indirect.

So, what's the problem then? Well, as you might have already figured out, it is in the realm of diagonals that conflict lies. Think about it. Expressives are very outgoing people. But if I (remember I am an Expressive) were to walk into my supervisors office, for example, and he happened to be an Analytical, and I slapped him on the shoulder, sat on the edge of his desk, and said, "What's up?" How do you think that might go over? Do you suppose that maybe, just maybe, there may be a tad of conflict between us?

Or, say a Driver is walking down the hallway and he's on a mission. He's got places to be and things to do. Along comes an Amiable walking the opposite direction. As they pass one another, the Amiable says, "Good morning, lieutenant. How are you doing today?" And the Driver? He says... nothing. Absolutely stone silent. He just keeps walking. Conflict? You betcha.

In fact, this example actually happened. I had a Driver lieutenant and an

Amiable officer do exactly as I described. It took me nearly two hours of "therapy" to convince the officer that LT didn't hate his guts! The moral of this story is that Amiables need to stop taking everything so personal, and Drivers -- for God's sake, stop ignoring your teddy bears; you're hurting their feelings.

14 COMMUNICATING WITH PERSONALITIES

So how exactly do we communicate with each personality type? It's easier than you might think.

COMMUNICATING WITH EXPRESSIVES

As I mentioned earlier, the Expressive motto is having fun. If you see a person walk into a room and you have that old Kool & The Gang song, "Celebrate good times, come on!" running through your head, you have just encountered an Expressive.

Now, the way you communicate effectively with an Expressive is to first make direct eye contact. Remember, these are very direct people, so it is important to show them you are connected. You accomplish this through looking them in the eye.

When speaking, you want to use a very energetic pitch. Speak relatively quickly, with a fast pace, and definitely allow time for socializing. Expressives love to know about you, and more importantly, they want you to know about them.

Always ask an Expressive about his or her intuition. Expressives are not big on planning usually. Their process is usually more flexible. They will try something, and if it doesn't work, they will try something else. And if that doesn't work? Try something else. And if that... well, you get the picture. Unlike an Analytical who plans every meticulous detail before implementing a course of action, an Expressive basically says, "Screw it, let's do it" and waits to see what happens, but because of their gifted intuition, they are usually more right than not.

Okay, this one is a biggie. You want to always, always support your ideas with testimonials from other people. Again, unlike Analyticals, Expressives are not big on facts and data. You could show an Expressive a stack of spreadsheets a foot high that details exactly how your idea will save the department a million dollars this year and he couldn't care less. More likely you will get a response like, "What does Bob think?" You see, he and Bob have a relationship. They've been friends since elementary school, and he trusts Bob's opinion much more than those spreadsheets.

It is important when dealing with Expressives to always balance achieving objectives with having fun. I've stated it before, if it ain't fun we ain't doing it.

And finally, if you really want to get on an Expressive's good side, talk about them. We're all closet narcissists.

COMMUNICATING WITH AMIABLES

As I alluded to earlier, Amiables are all about friendship. They absolutely love people.

When communicating with an Amiable, you want to make eye contact, but then you want to look away. A rough rule of thumb might be around three to five seconds of direct contact. Certainly no more than seven. In my experience, if you look directly at an Amiable for longer than seven seconds, you begin to freak them out a little. They start thinking, "Why is this person staring at me?" As a matter of fact, sometimes you can actually see a physical response. That's right, they will actually begin to lean back, unconsciously trying to create some distance between you and them.

Unlike an Expressive, with Amiables you want to slow down a bit, and speak with a more moderate pace and a much softer tone. And never, ever, EVER, use harsh language around an Amiable. Again, you will freak them out. (Side note: If you're in law enforcement, you most likely have Amiable officers in your department. This suggestion is a bit more flexible with them. Face it, if they've been on the street for longer than a week, they've likely heard -- or been called -- it all by now and have grown a bit numb to it.) If you ever need proof, accidently drop an F-Bomb in front of an elderly nurse and see what happens... she'll damn near have a heart attack!

If you find yourself disagreeing with an Amiable, you want to try and counter their argument with emotion more than with logic. Again, these are our teddy bears, and as such they tend to wear their hearts on their sleeves. They are heart people, not brain people. (No, I'm not implying that they're not smart, only caring.)

Remember the Bob example I gave regarding digging to get to their real concerns? You always want to allow time, and make the effort, to encourage them to express any doubts and concerns they may have. I warn you, it will take some real work on your part, but it will go a long way in establishing trust with this person in the future.

Likewise, you don't ever want to try to pressure an Amiable into making a decision. Give it time and let them come to their own conclusions naturally. It may take longer than you expect or like, but it's the only way to prevent them from retreating back into their shell. No pressure!

And finally, you should always try and mutually agree on things like goals, action plans, and time frames. Amiables are like Expressives in this area, and are not really detail oriented people. So you have to make sure that all parties involved are in agreement, otherwise you run the risk of offending them or hurting their feelings. And, as you probably know by now, they will never tell you that they were offended. They would rather just go away hurt than face confrontation in any way.

COMMUNICATING WITH ANALYTICALS

"Just the facts, Ma'am." You can almost hear Joe Friday utter those words in his trademark deadpan delivery every time you speak to an Analytical. As noted, their motto is give me only the facts and figures. You will typically find a lot of this personality type in careers such as engineering, accounting, lab technicians, etc.

When speaking to an Analytical you want to maintain a soft voice and speak at a fairly low volume. If you have ever seen Star Trek, think Mr. Spock. Notice he is rather formal with his speech, and even his physical mannerisms; you don't see a lot of flailing arms or gestures with him.

When pitching an idea to an Analytical you should always present the pros and the cons, and give them every option to consider. Part of what makes them analytical by nature is their habit of looking at a situation from all angles before making a decision. Oh, and don't ever overstate the benefits. If you promise them that your idea will save the department one million dollars this year, and on December 31st you have saved $999,999.98, the Analytical is going to want to know where his other .02 cents is! Okay, maybe they're not quite that bad, but close. Just remember to keep things real with them.

It's a good idea to follow up every interaction with an Analytical in writing. Chances are they are keeping a running log anyway, and this just helps them build a good paper trail. Details, details, details.

If you have a meeting scheduled, you certainly want to be on time. In fact, show up at least 10 minutes early if you can. They respect punctuality. Keep the meeting brief. Again, they don't like a lot of socializing and "fluff" -- just the facts. As I mentioned, you want to give them the pros and cons, and more importantly if you hope to get your idea accepted, show them how your plan has little or no risk. Analyticals are extremely risk adverse, and if you can show them how there is little down side to your approach, you'll get their support.

And finally, if you haven't grasped this point yet, be prepared to give them details... a LOT of details. We're talking data, graphs, numbers, analysis by experts, etc. This is how they make decisions, and if you don't give them enough to work with they will not go along with what you are asking simply by default.

COMMUNICATING WITH DRIVERS

If you've ever met a Driver, trust me, you'll know. They very much like to be in charge, and they have no problem letting everyone know it. If Drivers ever had a motto it would be this: Get it done, get it done right now, and get it done my way.

That's right. When working with a Driver, you could actually do everything correctly and achieve the right outcome and still be in conflict because you didn't do things exactly the way they would have done it.

When speaking to a driver you want to always make and maintain direct eye contact. Unlike the Amiable, you never want to look away when speaking. A Driver will interpret this as either a sign of disrespect, or at the very least will think you are hiding something. Drivers are strong people and they expect everyone else to be as strong as them. Therefore, it is somewhat ironic that when two or more Drivers get together there can be conflict because each typically wants to be in charge.

With Drivers you want to make sure you arrive on time, speak quickly, and use short sentences. In other words, they like to get down to business and have little patience for chit-chat. Be very specific and never over-explain or ramble on about things. And, as you might imagine, you want to focus on the outcome. One of the primary differences between an Analytical and a Driver is what each focuses on. For an Analytical it's all about the data. Data for a Driver is just a means to an end; for them, it's all about results.

And, last but most certainly not least, never, ever expect "warm fuzzies" from a Driver. It's simply not in their DNA. Does this mean that they won't give out a compliment? No. But in general, if they do, like anything else it's a means to an end. For example, if your supervisor is a Driver, he or she may have discovered along the way that people perform better if they feel good about themselves. And a good way to get people to feel good is to compliment them about their performance. It's not that they are insincere, but it does mean that the goal is better performance, not just to make you feel good.

STYLE STEPPING

So, now that you have learned how to recognize the various personality styles, and you know how to communicate with each one, what is the best way to reduce or eliminate conflict? It's a technique called style stepping.

My communication mentor, Dan O'Connor, states the idea is that when you are communicating with different types, you want to keep their personality in mind and "speak their language."

Here's an example. Let's say that you are an Expressive and you have a meeting scheduled with an Analytical. If you were to be yourself, you would clearly rub this person the wrong way. So what you do is style step. You literally shift gears, bring your personality down a notch or two, and -- in a sense -- become more of an Analytical. This way you are communicating in a manner and style that he or she is comfortable with. You are, in essence, speaking their language. And the more you practice style stepping the better you will become at it. Indeed, I have done it for so long now that it has become a form of muscle memory; I don't even think about it anymore. Once I recognize what type the other person is, I quickly mirror and match their personality practically automatically.

And you can, too.

15 TALKING TO THE EMOTIONALLY UPSET

"Emotionally upset" people are different from the difficult people you learned of earlier. Whereas a difficult person is one that is potentially angry and lashing out, an emotionally upset person is more quiet and reserved.

For instance, it might be a person who is quietly sitting in a chair with their face in their hands. Or someone leaning against the wall with their head tucked into their arm. They are not acting out in any way, but you can still tell there is clearly something on their mind. Naturally this would not be the time to walk up with our "Whoa, whoa, whoa... time out" Wedge. We need a much more subtle tool.

An excellent process I use goes back to our old friend, George Thompson. He referred to it as the LEAPS process.

LEAPS stands for:

Listen

Empathize

Ask

Paraphrase

Summarize

Let's break each one down into more detail, shall we?

LISTEN

The first step in dealing with an emotionally upset person is to listen. Now I know what you're thinking. That's easy. But is it really?

Stop for a minute and think about how most of us actually listen. Another person is speaking; and much of the time we are only "listening" just enough to pick up on a pause or something so we can jump in and say what it is we want to say.

Or, the person will say something and you immediately think of the perfect response. You've got a good one. I call these "zingers". The trouble is that your zinger is so good that you're afraid to forget it. So, you divert your focus to remembering it. And, of course, what happens to your listening skills if you are focused elsewhere? Exactly.

So, the key to effective listening is to actively listen to what they are saying. Active listening is much harder -- entire books have been written on the subject -- but the reward is worth it. I encourage you to do more research and work on your active listening skills, but for now one tip I can give you will help immediately.

Stop thinking about your response. Seriously. Don't focus on the zingers. Just pay attention to what the other person is saying as if you are going to have to repeat it back to them. Which, by the way, you will.

EMPATHIZE

Empathy is another one of these things that entire books have been written about. Indeed, many psychology programs in universities have numerous classes on the subject for their budding future therapists.

Perhaps the easiest way to demonstrate empathy for our purposes is to first put yourself in their shoes. Think to yourself, how would I feel if I were in the same situation? With that in mind, it is much easier to understand where this person's mind may be at the time.

On the outside, the most effective way to show empathy is through the use of common familiar responses.

"What?"

"Really?"

"You're kidding?"

"Mmmmmm..."

"I can't believe it."

"Oh!"

And so on. Comments like these should be fairly easy since we've all used them most of our lives. They are just those little interjections we throw out there now and then to show that we are paying attention and can relate to what it is they are going through.

Ask

Questions are often the key to any communication situation. Rather than giving you a million and one questions to memorize like a script, perhaps the easiest way to decide what questions to ask is to approach it like a good news reporter.

Just remember that almost all questions will fall into the basic pattern of who, what, where, when, why, and how. If you lead with some form of, "What's going on?" and then just follow the basic pattern after that, you will generally receive all of the information you may need.

There is one important warning I must mention, however. You must always ask questions relevant to their situation first. You only ask questions to obtain the information you need after you have gained a level of trust with this person.

If you begin peppering them with information questions (name, date of birth, address, etc.) too soon, you run the risk of your interaction coming across as more of an interrogation rather than an empathetic interview. In that case, they will come to believe that you don't really care about them, and that you are only trying to get the information you need to "fill out your stupid report so you can get back to your stupid sandwich." And, yes, that last part is in quotes because I have actually heard a person respond that way to a less-than-empathetic officer.

Paraphrase

In the paraphrase section, you are trying to feed back to the person the rough details of what they said. First, let's go over how it's done, and then we'll discuss why we do it.

Once a person has opened up to you a bit, and you've asked relevant questions, you want to give them back what they told you. I usually accomplish this through some variation of the following questions:

"Let me make sure I understand what you just said..."

"So, you're saying ______. Is that right?"

"I heard you say ______. Does that sound about right?"

Paraphrasing is an important step in the process because it does two very important things.

One, it ensures that you have the correct information. Naturally when you repeat back what a person said you will not do it word for word. But it is extremely important that you at least get the rough details correct. If you are relatively close, they will simply correct anything that is in error. However, trust me, if you feed back to the person something not even close you will find yourself shifting over to the Disturbance Set very quickly as they begin to escalate. And why would they escalate? Because you just proved you didn't care enough to listen.

Two, and more importantly, done correctly paraphrasing does a tremendous job of building trust and rapport with a person. You prove to them just how much you care because, quite honestly, most people don't respond with this level of empathy, so you will stand out in this person's life.

SUMMARIZE

Finally, we come to the summary.

Basically the summarize phase is merely a softer version of the Anchor technique you learned earlier. Once you have moved slowly through the LEAP portions of the process, you lock them down with a simple, "So what have we agreed to do?" or something similar.

The key here is to get the person's agreement on something -- anything -- that can possibly be seen as an improvement over their current state of mind. And it doesn't have to be anything grand. It literally could be as simple as the two of you agreeing that you would bring them a blanket or a cup of water, and they agreed to let you know if they need anything else.

It is important to understand that there is little to no pressure on your part. What I mean is that, at any point in this process, if the person chooses not to interact that it is entirely okay. Sometimes the best thing people need is just time.

Therefore, if the person says they are okay and they wish to be left alone at the moment, it is generally best to end the conversation with something like this:

"I understand. Well, my name is James, and I will be in the area for the rest of the evening. If there is anything I can do for you, or you just need someone to talk to, please don't hesitate to wave me down."

See? Just a simple I'm-here-if-you-need-me message. Also, note that I used my first name. When you are dealing with a difficult person who is acting up, you most likely want to maintain a "command" presence. Officer so-and-so and Sergeant such-and-such. With an emotionally upset person it is important that you come across as a caring human being, not as some kind of agent for the government.

I often take it a step further. There have been many occasions where I have sat beside the person, or even kneeled down in front of them to get to their eye level. In fact, I even remember a time that I laid on the floor beside a distraught mother who was proned out and in distress. Did it look funny? Probably. Did my uniform get a little dirty? Of course. Did I care? Not one bit. I'm too old to give a crap about what other people think about me, and uniforms can always be changed and washed. What's important is that I was there for that person when she needed someone the most.

16 THE POWER OF WORDS

I honestly cannot remember where I learned this next idea years ago, so forgive me for not citing a reference. Nevertheless, it is perhaps one of the best examples of the power of words I have ever come across.

I would like you read the following:

"I have some really good ideas that I would like to share. These ideas happen to inspire me, and I think you will want to listen so they will inspire you, too."

Now, here's the test. If I were to ask you three days from now if you could repeat those sentences from memory, could you do it? How about three weeks from now? Three months? Years?

What if I were to come up to you forty years from now and asked you to repeat what you read, do you think you would even remember what I am talking about much less the exact words?

But what If I were to change things up a bit? What if I were to reconfigure these sentences into what is known as a Power Phrase? Not only can I assure you that you would remember it forty years later, I can prove it.

What's the difference?

"I have some really good ideas that I would like to share. These ideas happen to inspire me, and I think you will want to listen so they will inspire you, too."

-OR-

"I have a dream."

Think about it. Isn't that exactly what Doctor King was saying with that statement? And yet, by speaking it as a Power Phrase, here we are some forty years after the fact and practically every single person in the United States past the third grade can cite it from memory.

That's the power of words. Sometimes a single word can make all the difference. Mark Twain once commented, "The difference between the right word and the almost right word is the difference between lightning and a lightning bug." I don't know about you, but I don't think I would notice much if I got hit in the chest by a lightning bug. Not sure if we can say the same about the other.

The Number One Method

Here's your assignment. Get yourself a little notebook. It doesn't need to be big; in fact, it's probably better if it's not because you will want to carry it with you at all times. This notebook is going to be your Danger/Power Phrase book.

How it works is you want to record phrases that you develop or overhear. Every time you say, or you hear someone else say, something that escalates a situation, that is what is known as a Danger Phrase. You want to make note of those so you don't use them in the future. Furthermore, you want to try and develop a Power Phrase to replace it. So what's a Power Phrase, you ask?

A Power Phrase is anything that you say, or that you hear someone else say, that deescalates a situation. It is critical that you record these Power Phrases, as the more you develop the more effective your communication skills become. In fact, this is by far the number one way to learn Tactical Communication.

Once you have recorded such Power Phrases, you absolutely must practice. Practice, and then practice some more. Practice at home in the mirror. Practice on your dog. I often joke that the Bluetooth headset was the best invention ever when it comes to communication skills, because in the old days if you walked down the street talking to yourself people thought you were crazy. Now they just think you're having a lively conversation!

So, no excuses. Record those phrases and get out there and practice.

Danger vs. Power

Here are a few Danger Phrases and Power Phrases to get you started. If you would like many more examples, please visit my friend Dan over at DanOConnorTraining.com. (By the way, I don't receive a dime from him if you do. I spent over a year going through his course and he is by far the best communicator I have ever seen; this is just my way of giving back. He actually doesn't even know I'm doing it.)

Danger Phrase: "What's wrong?"

Clearly there are times that we come across someone who is experiencing something wrong in their life. So, why do you suppose asking this would be a Danger Phrase?

The trouble with wording it this way is that when you say, "What's wrong?", people will generally tell you everything that is wrong with their life. An improved way to say the same thing is...

Power Phrase: "What's bothering you?"

This works much better. Typically, this question will illicit only the specific thing that is bothering the person at that moment.

For example, my partner and I once approached a woman who was being a tad disorderly. He starts out with, "What's wrong?" Of course, he should have known better because he had been through my class and, thus, I could have punched him in the head, but I digress.

Be that as it may, you know you are in for one hell of a ride when the conversation begins with, "Well, you see, me and my boyfriend was living in this single-wide when we was foreclosed on..." No less that fifteen minutes later we got to the crux of the problem and what was really bothering her. The Coke machine had taken her dollar.

Danger Phrase: "I understand how you feel."

Oh my goodness. If there were ever a shining example of how not to say something it is this. Think about it. When someone says to you, "I understand how you feel," what immediately pops into your head? Exactly. "You don't have a friggin' clue how I feel!" As a matter of fact, it doesn't even matter if you have gone through the exact same situation the day before and you truly do understand how they feel. If you say it, they simply will not believe you.

So, a much better way to say the same thing is by essentially tweaking just one word. Instead say...

Power Phrase: "I understand why you feel that way."

You see, by exchanging "how" for "why" you alter the entire meaning of the sentence. "I understand how you feel" means that you understand the emotions they are feeling inside and, as I mentioned, they won't agree. But by saying "I understand why you feel that way" you are essentially saying that you understand the chain of circumstances that led up to this moment.

It's a subtle difference, but a powerful one. One represents emotion, the other identifies events.

Danger Phrase: "You said..."

What's the trouble here? Quite simply, it puts the burden for any miscommunication on the other person. Believe it or not, I have observed situations where someone said, "You said..." and the other person replied, "No I didn't," even though the first person repeated exactly what they said word for word. Thus, the more effective way is to just reverse it...

Power Phrase: "I heard..."

This way, if there is any miscommunication, the burden is on you for not hearing correctly and there is much less chance for them to escalate.

Here's an oldie but a goody.

Danger Phrase: "Calm down."

In the history of man, dating all the way back to us swinging in trees and living in caves, has the phrase "Calm down" ever worked? I mean ever. I doubt it. It's just an ugly statement. Usually you'll get back some form of, "I am calm," while they shout, or, "Calm down? Whatchoo mean calm down?" Bottom line, it's just a bad way to go. Better is...

Power Phrase: "I can see how upset you are."

Now you are acknowledging and validating how the person feels. Also, if you do need an action word for some reason, such as "What I'm asking you to do is <action>," go with the word "relax". It means essentially the same thing as "calm down," but doesn't have 150,000 years of negative history behind it.

The final example is perhaps one of my biggest pet peeves.

Danger Phrase: "Our policy is..."

Ugh! I absolutely hate this phrase with a passion. It will basically get you the same response as calm down. The bottom line is that people don't really give two shits about what your policy is. Have you ever returned something to a store, only to have them not take it because their "policy" said something? How did it make you feel?

The trick to using this Power Phrase requires a bit of homework on your part. Have you ever known of a manager or executive that woke up in the morning, sat up in bed, stretched and yawned, and then said, "Hmmm... I think I'm going to make a policy today"? Of course not. That's not how these things work.

Why do we have policies in the first place? It's usually because some Einstein did something stupid, and we had to come up with a rule to ensure it doesn't happen again. So, your homework is to first discover what that rule is.

Next, you are going to state the rule or reason as a benefit statement. Only then do you explain the policy, but you never, ever, use the word "policy", you just simply say what it is. It works like this...

Power Phrase: "So that we can <benefit statement>, we only <policy>."

Here's an example. "Mr. Smith, so that we can ensure the safety of all our patients and guests, we only allow two visitors in the room at a time." What's the benefit statement? Ensuring everyone is safe. What's the policy? Only two visitors. But notice I never uttered the actual word "policy", it's just implied.

One quick tip before we move on. You absolutely must use this Power Phrase in order. Benefit first, then the policy statement. If you try and reverse them, you will never get to the benefit. They will most likely cut you off. For example,

"We only allow two visitors in the room at a time because..."

"I don't care what you allow. I want to see my son!"

See the difference?

Magic Phrases

Now let's talk about magic phrases.

Magic phrases are used when you need to gather more information or you need more clarity.

All of our magic phrases begin with the phrase, "that's interesting..." This is an excellent way to begin asking a magic phrase question.

The first magic phrase is, "tell me more." So, in practice it would sound something like this, "that's interesting, tell me more." As you can see this is an excellent way to get someone to open up and give you more information. Years ago, I was working as a manager in the restaurant industry. At the time, I was stationed in Nashville, Tennessee. I was required to fly back to Portland, Oregon for a manager's meeting. While on the plane, I met a traveling salesman named Bill. We exchanged pleasantries and I asked Bill what he did for a living. When Bill told me I said, "That's interesting, Bill, tell me more." From that point on every time Bill would stop talking I would simply say, "That's interesting, Bill, tell me more about that," and pick something he had said.

When Bill and I arrived at our destination to catch our connecting flights, before we went our separate ways Bill said to me, "you know James, it was really nice meeting you. In all of my years of travel I have never met a better conversationalist than you." Now, is that true? Am I really the best conversationalist Bill has ever met? Not really. You see, what really happened was for three hours Bill and I talked about Bill's favorite topic, which was... Bill. Any time you want to elicit more information from a person all you have to say is, "that's interesting, tell me more."

The next magic phrase is used when someone says something that you don't quite understand. When a person says something that you need clarification on you simply say, "That's interesting, why would you say that?"

For example, one time a young woman had stated that she wanted to commit suicide. But, here's the real question... Does anyone wake up in the morning and just randomly think to themselves, "I think I'm going to kill myself today"? Of course not. There are usually many reasons underlying that person's decision. What magic phrase number two does is help you discover those underlying reasons. So, when we arrived on the scene and the young woman stated that she wanted to commit suicide, if we were to deal with that statement would we have been dealing with the real problem? Instead, however, when she said she wanted to commit suicide I replied, "Why would you say that?" At that point she began to explain the underlying reason, and while addressing those reasons we were able to get her the help that she needed.

Before we get into magic phrase number three let me ask you a question: have you ever in your life said to a police officer, "Are you the real police?" Of course not. Why? Because you are a good guy (or girl). Who, then, asks this kind of question? Bad guys.

One of my biggest pet peeves is when I see officers go on the defensive. A suspect will throw something like that out and the officer responds with, "Well, of course I'm the real police. I've got the badge, I've got the gun, the patch on my sleeve says police, here's my patrol car..." What are you doing? When we stop a suspect and begin to question him, who is the spotlight on? The suspect, of course. But when we go on the defensive, who is the spotlight on? Us. And is that where the spotlight belongs? Of course not. So, when someone asks you a question that you don't quite understand, or you need more clarification, you use magic phrase number three.

"That's interesting, why would you ask me that?" Can you see how this works? In our scenario the suspect says, "Are you the real police?" And we reply with, "Why would you ask me that?" As you can see, we have now thrown the spotlight back on where it belongs.

Finally, magic phrase number four. One time I was on patrol and I saw a young man standing on the roof of a house. He had a towel wrapped around his neck like a cape and he was looking at a couple of bales of hay in the front yard. It doesn't take a genius to put two and two together and figure out what Superman is about to do. Well, because he was drunk at the time, he missed the bales of hay. After I approached and determined that he did not need medical treatment I asked, "That was interesting, why would you do that?" Any time someone does something that you don't quite understand use magic phrase number four. By the way, I had to look away to keep from laughing when he said it was because he just knew he could fly.

17 HOW TO HANDLE COMPLAINTS

If you have been in law enforcement or security for longer than about 30 seconds you know that a big part of our job is dealing with complaints. And, many times the complaints are not even about us. For example, it is quite common where I work to hear a complaint like, "That staff member was mean to me."

The best method I have learned for dealing with complaints is what I call the VCR technique. Here we want to validate, commit, and reveal and resolve. Yes I know this spells VCRR, but it's my book so it's my joke.

Step number one is to validate their feelings. This is really simple. An excellent way to do this is:

"Mr. and Mrs. Jones, I can see why you're upset by all of this, and I don't blame you. I do apologize for any trouble you've been through." A statement like this is usually very effective because often people are not even looking for a solution, per se, but just someone to listen. While it's not common, I have even experienced situations where I did not need to go beyond step one. Just by validating the person's feelings they were satisfied with the result. However, for purposes of training let's assume we need to go on.

Step number two is to reinforce your commitment. Notice I said your commitment. Not your department and not your chief. Your commitment. You want to convey the idea that you will be solving their challenge personally, because if a person brings a complaint to you and you say, "You should really tell so-and-so about this." Well, who is so-and-so? You see, at this point you are the only representative that this person knows. Don't be lazy and try to pass the buck to some phantom entity. This is all about your commitment. The way to do this is fairly simple: "That said, I'm committed to seeing you through this."

The final step is to reveal your contact information (and resolve their problem, of course.) Here you simply say:

"My name is officer Wayne. My phone number is 555-5555. My email address is BruceWayne@GothamPD.gov. If you just give me a chance, I know that I can get this resolved for you. Would you let me try?"

Notice the, "Would you let me try?" part. See how this is just a different version of our anchor technique from earlier. Putting it all together it goes something like this:

"Mr. and Mrs. Jones, I can see why you're upset by all of this, and I don't blame you. I apologize for any trouble you've been through. That said, I'm committed to seeing you through this. My name is officer Jones. My phone number is 555-5555 and my email address is BruceWayne@GothamPD.gov. If you just give me a chance, I know that I can get this resolved for you. Would you let me try?"

Now if you were to go through these three steps what are the chances when you get to, "Would you let me try?" that this person would reply with, "No!"? It wouldn't happen, right? I have used this technique repeatedly for years now and it almost always works.

So, you have this person's complaint. Now what do you do? Let's pretend that the complaint is a football. Who's holding the football now? You are, of course. Whose football is it? It's yours. After all, you are the one that gave this person your commitment. Now it is here where I sometimes get pushback from younger officers. I will hear things like, "But, Sarge, I am just a lowly rookie officer. How am I going to solve such a big problem?" Here is the key...

We have established that it is your football. But that does not mean that you can't bring the football to a more senior officer. So, you bring the problem to Cpl. Smith and say, "I have this huge football." Is it Cpl. Smith's job to take the football? No. But, Cpl. Smith may help you find the solution. But let's say that he doesn't know. So you take the football to Sgt. Adams. Can you give the football to Sgt. Adams? I'm sure by now you know the answer. And, for the sake of argument, let's say Sgt. Adams doesn't know the answer either. So you take the football to the lieutenant, the captain, the major, the assistant chief, or even to the chief himself. None of these are going to take the football, but they will help you find a solution, at which point it is your responsibility to take the answer back to the person you spoke to.

There are two things you need to be aware of at this point. One, what if you recognize that this is a big "football" and it's going to take some time to resolve. Is it okay to tell the person? Of course. The key is to give them a reasonable explanation and timeline. You would simply say, "Mr. Jones, this is quite the challenge, and it may take some time to resolve. I am going to need to get several other people involved. Having said that, you have my commitment – can I get your phone number, sir? – You have my commitment that I will call you Thursday morning at 10 AM and let you know where I'm at on this. Sound good?" The key here is that you live up to your commitment, which means that Thursday morning at 10 AM (or whatever time you've agreed to) you will call Mr. Smith back with either an answer or simply to check in. "Mr. Jones, this is officer Wayne. I was just calling to let you know that I hadn't forgotten about you and I'm still working on finding you a solution."

The second important point to be aware of is that there may come a time where the solution you and others come up with may not be exactly what they were looking for. Is this still okay? Yes.

And here's why...

Let's say that you call Mr. Jones on Thursday and deliver the "bad" news. Now, think carefully before answering this. Is Mr. Jones likely to be disappointed? Of course he will. However, is Mr. Jones likely to be upset? In my experience, the answer is no. While Mr. Jones may not like the answer, I have found that he will still appreciate all of the effort that you took to try to take care of him. And though I have no proof, my belief is that it's because no one is providing this level of customer service in today's fast-paced world. The fact that you have shown interest and that you cared enough to put that kind of effort into helping this person goes a long, long, way today.

18 YOUR PERSONAL COMPASS

What do we use a compass for? A compass is used to find direction. So, what do you think we use a personal compass for? To find direction in our lives, of course. The way to use a personal compass is to ask yourself, "What am I here to do?" For this I don't mean what you are here to do as a law enforcement officer. Think bigger than that. What are you here to do as a human being on this planet? Next, you want to create a list of "I am..." statements. For example, I am patient, I am kind, I am compassionate, etc.

Step number two in the personal compass is to ask yourself, "What am I here to do?" Again, I don't mean here in your job or your department. I mean what are you here on this planet to do? Like before you want to create a list of "I am here to..." statements. For example, "I am here to have fun and enjoy life." Or, "I am here to provide knowledge and life skills my students need to be happy, productive and fulfilled in their journey." Create a series of statements that outline what you feel your purpose is on this planet.

So why is a personal compass important? I learned this technique from my friend, Dan O'Connor. And Dan puts it this way:

"If you come from who you are, the words will take care of themselves."

In this book you have learned a lot of new techniques. And I have given you a lot of tools. I encourage you to memorize and practice the tools, techniques, and scripts that you have learned. It is a lot like muscle memory when you learn to shoot. The goal in firearms training is to get to the point where you don't have to think about it. If something happens that requires you to pull your weapon you simply do it without consciously thinking about it. Tactical Communication requires this same kind of training. The only difference is the muscle we're talking about here is your tongue. You want to get to the point where you know these scripts and these tools so well that you can answer with a proper response unconsciously. However, as Dan noted, if you have a strong enough personal compass you are already there. Because if you are a kind and compassionate person, script or not, how are you likely to respond to a person? With kindness and compassion, of course. If what you are here to do is to bring joy to others, or to provide outstanding customer service, how are you likely to respond to that person?

Years ago, when I was working in sales, I attended a seminar by the immortal

Zig Ziglar, and he made a statement that has stuck with me for nearly 30 years:

"People don't care how much you know, until they know how much you care."

At the beginning of my live classes I give the students my resume, and I'll be honest, I lay it on fairly thick. I talk about my education, how I have more letters behind my name than in my name, and about how I have more degrees than a thermometer. I may have even mentioned that I have an IQ of 146 a time to two. But it's not because I'm trying to look like Mr. Big Shot. I set up all of that for this moment...

While all of that may be true, I always tell my students that my resume plus $6.95 gets me a latte at Starbucks. In other words, absolutely nothing. Because at the end of the day, if you were my partner and you were in trouble, would you really care how many degrees I have? Would you give a rat's butt about what my IQ is? Or, when it really hits the fan, would the only thing you care about is how much I care about you? What would you consider more important? A fancy resume or the fact that I would take a bullet to make sure you go home to see your family? People don't care how much you know, until they know how much you care. I hope by now you can see just how much I care.

Now I encourage you to go forward with that same kind of spirit. And not just for those you work with or your family. Let's face it; it is really easy to get caught up in the negativity of this job. Let's say, for example, you are involved in a situation where our stereotypical gang banger from earlier has been shot, and because the negativity of this job has jaded you, you think to yourself, "Well, he got what he deserved." Now of course you would never say this out loud, but you still think it. Now what happens when his mother arrives? Who does she see lying there? Does she see a 20-year-old gang banger? Does she see a drug dealer? No. In her mind she sees her baby. And of course you don't say to her that he got what he deserved, but do you think she still knows what you're thinking? Of course she does, because it's written all over your face and she can hear it in your voice.

People don't care how much you know, until they know how much you care. Make sure they know it. Good luck, and be safe.